THE TABLETOP LEARNING SERIES

DINOSAURS

Facts, Fun, and Fantastic Crafts

by Imogene Forte

Incentive Publications, Inc.
Nashville, Tennessee

Illustrated by Susan Eaddy
Cover illustrated by Becky Cutler
Ideas contributed by Sue Reinhardt
Edited by Sally Sharpe

Library of Congress Catalog Number 86-82932
ISBN-0-86530-149-2

THE TABLETOP LEARNING SERIES™ is a trademark of Incentive Publications, Inc.,
Nashville, TN 37215

THIS
DINOSAUR BOOK
BELONGS TO

_____

CONTENTS

DINO-INFO

A NOTE TO KIDS

Take a trip back in time to the intriguing prehistoric world of the dinosaurs! All you need is a little free time and this book. You'll learn about the fascinating creatures who inhabited the earth millions of years ago as you enjoy hours of creative learning fun! All of the projects and activities are easy to do and are lots of fun. Some are for you to complete individually and others are for you to do with a friend or even with a group of friends!

The DINO-CRAFTS section is full of easy-to-make dinosaur craft projects. You will find papier-mâché projects, collages, sculptures, mobiles, and many other creative crafts. All you need are easy-to-find materials and a little imagination to make your prehistoric friends come to life!

In the DINO-FUN section you'll find great ideas for throwing your very own dinosaur party. There are activities for making invitations, preparing party treats, and planning "dino-mite" party games! You will never be without a fun dinosaur idea.

The DINO-INFO section gives you messages to decode, games to play, puzzles to solve, and mazes to work. Each activity is packed with interesting information about dinosaurs and their world. When you're through with this section, you're sure to be a dinosaur wizard!

So, organize your supplies, choose your first dinosaur activity, and get ready for a fun learning adventure!

DINO-RHYME
I

Today there are no more dinosaurs, no not even **one**,
   but studying all about them is really lots of _____ !

Dinosaur means "terrible lizard", try hard not to **forget**,
   they lived when the world was very warm and also very _____ .

Many dinosaurs dined on plants and some would just have **meat**,
   one "dino" was as big as a house, think how much he'd _____ .

There's much to learn about dinosaurs right inside this **book,**
some things to make and games to play, why don't you take a _____!

You will learn, you will create and you will have lots of **laughs,**
so start with section I, it's full of dinosaur _____!

Gosh, look at those spikes.

I wonder if he eats cats.

wet

crafts

eat

look

fun

Polacanthus

HATCHING IT OUT

*dinosaurs were hatched from eggs -- some were big and some were small,
some eggs were the size of a potato and some the size of a football!*

BABIES

papier mâché shells for two baby dinosaurs

WHAT TO USE:

- large bowl or other container
- newspaper
- water
- flour (about 2-3 cups)
- scissors
- cream-colored paper or paint
- potato and plastic football or objects of like size

WHAT TO DO:

1. Put the flour in a bowl and add water slowly. Mix until a smooth paste forms.
2. Cut newspaper into strips about 1½ inches wide.
3. Spread other newspaper on the work space to keep it neat.
4. Cover both sides of each strip with the paste.
5. Apply the strips to the objects. Cover each object completely and then add another layer.

6. If you have cream-colored paper, use this for the outside layer. If not, paint your "eggs" after the paste has dried completely. (It may take a day for the papier-mâché to dry. Be sure to wait!)

7. Using scissors or a knife, carefully cut a zigzag line around the eggs. Gently remove the objects from the papier-mâché shell.

WHAT IS FUN:
Trace the two baby dinosaurs on page 14. Color them with markers or crayons and cut them out. Put the dinosaurs inside their shells as if they were hatching!

STICKY STEGOSAURUS
another papier-mâché activity!

I've got long back legs and a bird-like head,
I have bony plates on my back,
And with papier-mâché & talent like yours,
You can make me from a paper sack!

WHAT TO USE:
- large bowl or other container
- newspaper (lots of it!)
- water
- flour (about 2-3 cups)
- scissors
- paper sack
- string
- masking tape
- paint
- paintbrush
- shellac (optional)

WHAT TO DO:
1. Fill the paper sack with wadded newspaper. Tie a piece of string around the opening of the sack to make the dinosaur's body.
2. To make the legs, tightly roll pages of newspaper. (The legs must be rolled very tightly so they will be strong enough to hold up your Stegosaurus.)

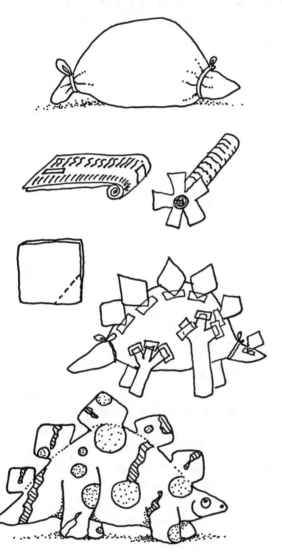

3. Cut one end of each "leg" to make flaps for attachment.
4. Tape the flaps securely to the body.
5. Fold newspaper into several thick squares and fold over one corner of each square.
6. Tape the folded corners to the dinosaur's back to make bony plates. *Note:* Follow the directions for making paste and preparing strips as outlined in BABIES, page 15.
7. Cover the entire Stegosaurus with papier-mâché.
8. After it has completely dried (a day or two), paint your creature or shellac it for a shiny look. *Note:* Most dinosaurs are believed to have been green or brown, but it's your choice! Don't worry if your sculpture doesn't look exactly like a Stegosaurus. You may create a whole new look for dinosaurs! Paint and decorate your Stegosaurus as you choose!

PERKY PTERANODON

Pteranodon was a high flyer -- its wings spanned 25 feet,
it lived atop towering sea cliffs -- and scooped up fishes to eat.
A bony crest on back of its head -- and legs that were quite weak,
Pteranodon was replaced by birds -- and one day became extinct!

WHAT TO USE:

- light cardboard such as poster board
- tracing paper
- pencil

- scissors
- glue or tape
- crayons or markers
- string

WHAT TO DO:

1. Trace the patterns on pages 21 and 22 and then cut them out.
2. Put the cut-out patterns on the cardboard, trace around them, and cut out the cardboard pieces. (Remember to make two wings.)
3. Decorate the Pteranodon however you would like.
4. Fold and slit the cardboard parts as shown in the illustration.

You hold it down & I'll trace it.

5. Fit the pieces together and glue or tape them where necessary.
6. Run the string through the slit on the Pteranodon's back. Knot the end or tape it securely.

WHAT IS FUN:
Make several Pteranodons to create a prehistoric mobile for you or your baby brother or sister.

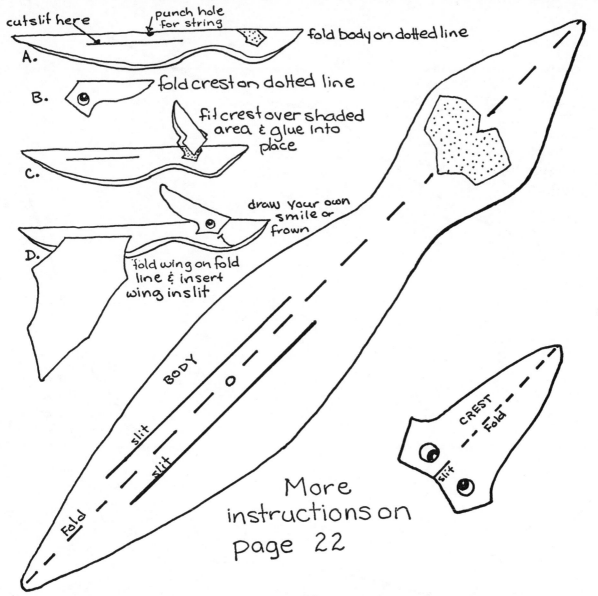

cut slit here

punch hole for string

fold body on dotted line

A.

B.

fold crest on dotted line

fit crest over shaded area & glue into place

C.

draw your own smile or frown

D.

fold wing on fold line & insert wing in slit

BODY

slit

slit

Fold

CREST

Fold

slit

More instructions on page 22

21

E.

Tape together the inside flaps of the wings after they're inserted into the body.

cut 2 wings

Fold flap downward

Front

insert string through hole & knot on underside

F.

SHAPE-O-SAURUS

rectangles, triangles, and circles galore,
assemble a creature with these shapes and more!

WHAT TO USE:
- poster board or cardboard
- construction paper
- glue
- scissors
- crayons, markers, or paint

WHAT TO DO:
1. Cut out different shapes from construction paper. (If you fold the paper, you can cut two or three shapes at a time.) Use lots of different colors.
2. Glue the shapes onto the cardboard to make a dinosaur.
3. Draw background scenery to show the creature's environment.

Fold paper in ½ or in quarters

Some shapes you can make

PUZZLING POLACANTHUS

this dinosaur was a plant eater --
his spikes guarded him from attack,
try scrambling the puzzle pieces,
and then try to put each one back!

WHAT TO USE:
- cardboard box with top (small shirt box is good)
- flat piece of cardboard (about the size of the bottom of the box)
- tracing paper
- glue or tape
- scissors
- markers or crayons

WHAT TO DO:
1. Trace the outline of the Polacanthus on this page and then cut out the pattern.
2. Trace around the pattern on the inside of the bottom of the box.

you could color
his spikes purple.

1

BOX TOP

2

I have to use my pocket knife
to get this cutout started.

Be careful...
I'll finish
cutting it
out with
my scissors.

3

I'll glue this cardboard
to the back of the box...

while
I cut along
the puzzle
lines

3. Color the dinosaur any color you like.
4. Now, draw puzzle lines on the dinosaur with a dark marker. (Remember to keep the puzzle simple. A puzzle that is too confusing is not fun.)
5. Cut out the outline of the Polacanthus. Then, cut along the puzzle lines to make the pieces.
6. Turn the box over and glue the flat piece of cardboard to the bottom of the box.

WHAT IS FUN:

Use a stopwatch or count to see how long it takes you to put the puzzle together. Try to improve your speed each time you work the puzzle.

Hey! Not bad!

We make
a pretty
good
team.

4

ANIMATE ANATOSAURUS

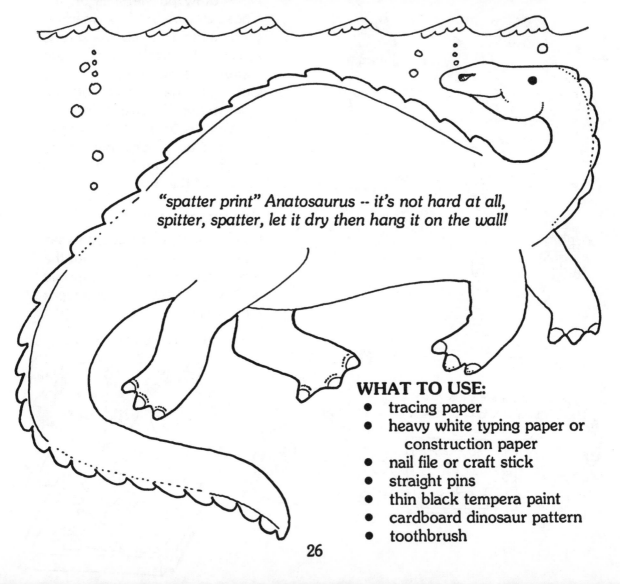

*"spatter print" Anatosaurus -- it's not hard at all,
spitter, spatter, let it dry then hang it on the wall!*

WHAT TO USE:
- tracing paper
- heavy white typing paper or construction paper
- nail file or craft stick
- straight pins
- thin black tempera paint
- cardboard dinosaur pattern
- toothbrush

WHAT TO DO:

1. With tracing paper over the Anatosaurus pattern on page 26, trace the outline of the dinosaur's body. Cut out the pattern.
2. Pin the pattern to the center of a piece of white paper.
3. Dip the toothbrush in the paint, being careful not to get too much paint.
4. Using the nail file or craft stick, scrape the bristles of the toothbrush so the paint will spatter onto the pattern.
5. Let the paint dry completely.
6. Take out the pins and remove the pattern. Your Anatosaurus "spatter print" is now ready for display!

A PILLOW-SAURUS

for play or rest

Fold the right sides together.

I'll pin on the pattern & you can cut it out.

First you cut out the 2 pieces

Then you sew them together

remember, the wrong side faces out!

WHAT TO USE:

- brown paper bag
- fabric
- cotton, old nylon stockings or other stuffing
- scissors
- needle and thread
- buttons, yarn, braid or rickrack

WHAT TO DO:

1. Draw an outline of your favorite dinosaur on one side of a brown paper bag.
2. Cut out the outline to make a pillow pattern.
3. Fold the fabric in half with the right sides together. Pin the pattern to the fabric and cut around it to make two pieces.
4. With the right sides of the two pieces of fabric together, use needle and thread to sew the pieces together around the edges. Be sure to leave an

opening for the stuffing. Make small stitches to sew the pieces together, and then go back over the stitches a second time so the pillow will be tight enough to hold the stuffing.

5. Turn the pillow inside out so that the right side of the fabric is showing.
6. Stuff the pillow with the material of your choice.
7. Sew the opening together.
8. To finish the pillow, make a face and other features using buttons, yarn, and other trim.

Turn the pillow right side out & stuff it

Then sew up the opening

Why Brock! What a nice gift!

For me? Bruno! what a surprise!

Aw, Shucks... I couldn't have done it without Brock's help.

CIRCLE-O-SAURUS

WHAT TO USE:
- poster board or cardboard
- construction paper
- circular lids of various sizes
- glue
- scissors
- crayons, markers, or paint

WHAT TO DO:
1. Put the lids on construction paper and trace them.
2. Cut the circles out of the construction paper and glue them onto the cardboard to make a dinosaur.
3. Draw background scenery to give the beast a home.

DINO-SOAP

WHAT TO USE:
- leftover soap pieces
- water

WHAT TO DO:
1. Gather leftover soap pieces. (Friends and relatives might be able to contribute!)
2. Soak the soap pieces in water until they are soft enough to mold.
3. Choose your favorite pattern on this page and mold the soap in the shape of that dinosaur.
4. Allow the soap to harden before moving the sculpture.

WHAT IS FUN:
Make several prehistoric creatures. Stage dinosaur battles in the warm, wet world of your bathtub ... but don't forget to wash!

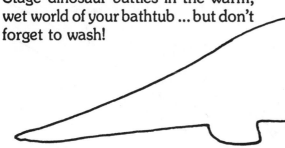

TUBE-O-SAURUS

create some very special features --
glue them to your cardboard creatures!

WHAT TO USE:

- cardboard tubes of all sizes
- construction paper
- paper plates
- glue or tape
- scissors

glue or tape tubes
together

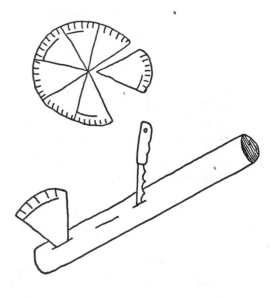

You can crumple the end of one tube & insert it in another tube. Tape it together if you need to

WHAT TO DO:

1. Cover the tubes with construction paper (optional).
2. Glue the tubes together to make a prehistoric creature.
3. Cut out sections of paper plates to use as bony plates.
4. Make slits in the tubes along the creature's back and insert the bony plates.
5. Make special features by cutting out shapes from construction paper and gluing them on the creature.

make a slit in bottom tube, flatten small tube, insert, & bend to make feet. tape in place if you need to...

crumple tube & insert

then bend

BOX-O-SAURUS

use boxes of every size

WHAT TO USE:
- 1 big box
- toothpicks
- smaller boxes of
  different sizes

- glue or tape
- scissors
- markers
- paint (optional)

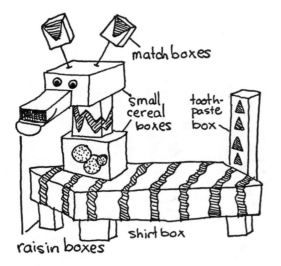

match boxes

small cereal boxes

tooth-paste box

raisin boxes

shirt box

WHAT TO DO:
1. Glue the boxes together to make a creature.
2. Use toothpicks to attach smaller boxes for features such as horns, tails, or ears. You might like to give your creature spikes by sticking toothpicks in the boxes.
3. Use the markers to draw other special features.
4. You can finish your creature by giving it a coat of paint.

COLLAGE-O-SAURUS

WHAT TO USE:
- large sheet of sturdy cardboard
- markers
- scissors
- glue
- waxed paper
- egg cartons, scraps of fabric, buttons, sandpaper, candy wrappers, cotton balls, and other assorted materials

WHAT TO DO:
1. Draw the outline of a dinosaur on the cardboard.
2. Cut the egg carton apart to form individual cups.
3. Crumple the waxed paper into balls.
4. Begin filling in the dinosaur's body by gluing on the egg carton cups and crumpled waxed paper balls. Add scraps of fabric, candy wrappers, buttons, sandpaper, cotton balls, and other "junk" items to completely cover the body surface.
5. Give the dinosaur a face by gluing on similar materials for the eyes, nose, mouth, and tongue. Remember, this dinosaur is a friendly fellow, so give him a face to match his disposition!

DINO-RHYME
II

*Dinosaurs were hatched from eggs -- many were laid in the **sand**, some of the eggs were small enough to fit in the palm of your _____ !*

*Some dinosaurs had many teeth, I would not want to **count**, and some had plates upon their backs to ward off an enemy's _____ .*

Look at all those eggs!

Look at all those dinosaurs!

King

38

Remember: the words at the end of each line must rhyme.

Sharp horns and spikes were used, by dinosaurs heavy and **slow**,
  when one "dino" sensed danger, under water he would _____ !

Using sharp teeth and strong legs, or even taking to **wing**,
  dinosaurs protected themselves, from the smallest to
  the _____ .

To learn more about dinosaurs, this is what you must **do**,
  get ready for tons of more "dino-fun", here in **section II**!

go

hand   mount

THROW A DINO-PARTY

Dinosaur lovers throughout the nation --
   get ready for a fun celebration,
It's "dino" PARTY time, so clap your hands,
   there's fun ahead for all dinosaur fans!

Dinosaur refreshments are in this book,
   just flip through the pages and take a look,
Prehistoric punch and fossils to cook,
   so now grab your apron off of the hook!

Fun dinosaur games are in store for you,
*   a "follow-me" friend tells you*
*   what to do.*
Pin the tail on Allosaurus, that's some-
*   thing new,*
A "dino" word game is included, too!

But before you start your celebration,
*   you'll need to design an invitation.*
With good ideas and anticipation,
*   Plan your party without procrastination!*

Oh, Bruunnooo...
Come see what
I have for you...

I feel ridiculous.

I'm glad they
didn't dress
me up.

41

DINO-PARTY INVITATION

a real "stand-out"

WHAT TO USE:
- white paper, 8½ inches by 11 inches
- markers or crayons
- scissors
- pencil

WHAT TO DO:
1. Fold a piece of paper in half.
2. Choose one of the dinosaur patterns in this book and trace it onto one half of the paper. (Remember to keep the dinosaur's feet near the open side of the paper.)
3. Color and decorate the dinosaur as you like.
4. Trim the paper following the dinosaur's outline to give the invitation a unique shape, but keep the bottom edge straight so that the dinosaur will stand up.

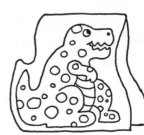

You're invited to a DINO-PARTY ◇·◇·◇

Given by _____
Date _____
Time _____
Place _____
RSVP # _____

5. Write the important party information inside the invitation as shown.

42

WHAT IS FUN:
When all the invitations are finished, put them in stamped envelopes and mail them to your "dinosaur-loving" friends!

an easy-to-make envelope

WHAT TO USE:
- white paper
- scissors
- glue

WHAT TO DO:
1. Fold the bottom of a piece of paper 2/3 of the way to the top.
2. Glue the side edges together to make a pocket.
3. Cut triangle sections out of the sides of the top flap as shown.
4. Insert the invitation and fold down the flap.
5. Glue the flap to the pocket, address and stamp the envelope, and deliver the invitation to the nearest mailbox!

DINOSAUR LOOK ALIKE

Dino-who? Why, it's only you!

WHAT TO USE:
- a big box
- large shoe box (or boot box)
- scissors
- paint, markers, crayons, glue
- "junk"

WHAT TO DO:
1. Carefully cut holes in the big box for your head, arms, and legs. Make the holes large enough so that you can move freely.
2. Standing in front of a mirror, try on the box. Think about how you can decorate the box so that you will look like a dinosaur.
3. Take off the box. Use paint, markers, and any good "junk" you can find to decorate the body of your costume.
4. Take the top off of the shoe box and fit the box over your head. With a marker or crayon, mark holes for your eyes, nose and mouth.

Tie on box with string or elastic

Here, let me mark the eyeholes

5. Carefully cut out the holes so that you will be able to see, breathe and talk.
6. Paint and decorate the mask to match your dinosaur "body".

WHAT IS FUN:
Collect enough boxes, scissors, markers, glue and good "junk" materials for your party guests to make "dino-who" costumes. Making the costumes will be fun, but marching in a "dino-parade" will be even more fun!

yarn

rowwrrr!

grrrr!

45

DINO-T-SHIRTS

make a dinosaur T-shirt in your very own home --
wear your dinosaur friend wherever you roam!

WHAT TO USE:
- white paper
- crayons
- white T-shirt
- clothes iron

WHAT TO DO:
1. Draw a dinosaur on a piece of paper, or trace one of the patterns in this book. Go back over the drawing with crayons, pressing hard so that the colors are bold and bright. (Remember: anything you draw or write will be transfered **reversely** onto the shirt!)
2. Put the paper, crayon side down, on the shirt.
3. Set the iron's heat selector for your chosen fabric.
4. With an adult's supervision, slowly iron the piece of paper, allowing the crayon to "melt" into the shirt.

That's right, Elliot; crayon side down.

5. Let the paper cool and then remove it to unveil your dinosaur.
6. Clean the crayon pieces off the iron with a wet sponge while the iron is still warm.

WHAT IS FUN:

Encourage your friends to make their own T-shirts. Start a dinosaur club and wear your shirts to the first party!

NEAT —

Always unplug the iron before you clean it.

I'M A DINO-MITE DAD

ELLIOT

PREHISTORIC PUNCH

WHAT TO USE:
- 1 big glass
- 1 tablespoon molasses
  or maple syrup
- ½ cup cold milk
- peppermint stick
- ginger ale or club soda
- 1 big scoop chocolate
  ice cream

WHAT TO DO:
1. Pour the molasses or syrup into the glass.
2. Pour in ½ cup of milk.
3. Add the scoop of ice cream.
4. Pour in enough ginger ale or soda to fill up the glass.
5. Stir the mixture with the peppermint stick and then sip, sip, sip through
   the peppermint stick.

SEDIMENT SLUSH

If you layer these ingredients in glasses according to the directions below, you will have imitations of the layers of sediment that covered the earth during the time of the dinosaurs.

WHAT TO USE:
- 1 box instant vanilla pudding
- 8 medium-sized glasses
- 1 quart milk
- 2 bowls
- measuring cup
- 1 box instant chocolate pudding
- vanilla wafers (or other cookies)
- spoon

WHAT TO DO:
1. Mix each flavor of pudding with two cups of milk, using a separate bowl for each flavor, according to the package directions.
2. Break several vanilla wafers into small chunks. Break the remaining cookies to make crumbs.
3. Pour a layer of chocolate pudding in each glass.
4. Top the pudding in each glass with a layer of the vanilla wafer chunks and cookie crumbs.
5. Pour a layer of vanilla pudding over the wafer layer.
6. Continue layering the pudding and wafers until all of the ingredients have been used.

They call it sediment slush

BAKE A GINGER-SAURUS

stir and bake a special treat --
it's fun to make and good to eat!

WHAT TO USE:

- scissors
- tracing paper
- cardboard
- 1 package gingerbread mix
- spatula
- several tablespoons
- large mixing spoon
- table knife
- large baking sheet
- rolling pin or a smooth glass
- butter or shortening
- any of the following: raisins, almonds, chocolate bits, gumdrops
- flour

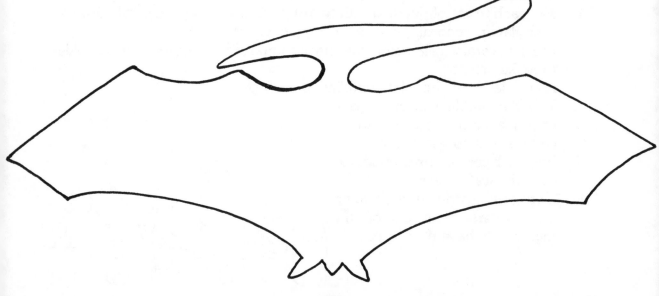

use a fork
to make
patterns
on fin
before baking

WHAT TO DO:

1. Trace the dinosaurs on these two pages and cut them out to make patterns.

2. Place the patterns on cardboard and trace around them. Now, cut out the cardboard patterns.

3. Grease the baking sheet with butter or shortening.

4. Pour the gingerbread mix into a bowl and add enough water to make a stiff dough. (Be careful not to add too much!)

5. Divide the dough into three balls. Using the rolling pin, roll out each dough ball on a floured surface.

6. Place the cardboard dinosaur patterns on the dough and carefully cut around them with a knife to make cookies. (Cut as many cookies as you can.)

7. Use the spatula to place the dinosaur cookies about ½ inch apart on the baking sheet.

8. Decorate the cookies with any of the "goodies" mentioned on the previous page. Give some cookies friendly faces, some fearful eyes, and others spiked backbones.

9. Bake your creatures according to the directions on the gingerbread package.

FOSSIL BITES

for refreshment only!

WHAT TO USE:
- refrigerated sugar cookie dough
- flour
- rolling pin or a smooth glass
- round cookie cutter or jar lid
- fork, plastic knife, seashells, wire screen, and other objects for imprinting

WHAT TO DO:
1. Roll out the cookie dough on a clean, smooth surface. (Use pinches of flour as necessary to prevent sticking.)
2. When the dough has been flattened, use a cookie cutter or jar lid to cut out the "fossil" cookies.

3. Use various objects to make impressions in the cookie dough. (Remember to press hard so the imprint will still be there after the dough rises!) Fossils can be shells, teeth, horns, claws, bones, or whole animals! Try molding pieces of cookie dough into some of these objects.

4. Sprinkle your "fossils" with sugar to make "rocks" that are sweet to eat.

5. Bake the cookies according to the directions on the sugar cookie package or recipe.

wire screen

molded dough

seashells

plastic fern

THREE QUICK AND EASY DINOSAUR GAMES

I am Thinking of a Dinosaur
A player begins the game by saying "I am thinking of a dinosaur". After describing the dinosaur, in *three sentences only*, the player asks the others to guess the dinosaur's name. The player who correctly names the dinosaur takes the next turn and does the same thing. The game continues until all players have had a turn or until the group cannot think of any other dinosaurs!

this dinosaur is as big as a football field

Dinosaur Words
Each player will need pencil and paper. The object of the game is for each player to try to make the longest list of words which begin with the letters in the word **dinosaur**. The players agree upon the time limit before the game begins. When the time is up, the player with the longest list of words is the winner.

54

This Dinosaur Says . . .

This game is a lot like "Simon Says" and is a good way to "get a party going". The game is not as easy as it seems, but requires concentration and good listening skills. One player is chosen to be "it". He or she stands before the group and gives directions such as "this dinosaur says roll over three times like a Stegosaurus", or "this dinosaur says sit down like a Brontosaurus". The catch is to listen for the dinosaur name in each direction. In other words, the person who is "it" will always say "this dinosaur says..." but will not always say "like a _____ " (using a dinosaur name). Players who follow the directions without a dinosaur name are out of the game. The last player who is still in the game becomes "it" and starts a new game.

This dinosaur says turn upside down.

TALL TALES TO TELL AND ENJOY!

For a sure-to-entertain game, select one of the following "story starters" and ask your friends to take turns adding to the story. Continue developing the story until everyone has had a turn or until someone gives the story an exciting ending.

When our teacher asked us to make dinosaur costumes for the school parade, she never expected such a strange thing to happen. It all began when Jimmy . . .

Imagine my surprise when I opened the door and found a stegosaurus standing on my front porch. The first thing I did was . . .

"Help!" called the museum night watchman as he walked into the dinosaur room. All of the skeletons were swaying to the beat of mysterious, eerie music. Suddenly, he . . .

The radio broadcaster made the announcement at high noon. A brontosaurus had just been spotted thumping down 5th avenue in New York City. Cars were running off the streets, people were . . .

TAILS FOR ALLOSAURUS

a good game for the "tail end" of a party!

Allosaurus, a swiftly-moving reptile with a long, heavy tail, often has been called the "dragon dinosaur".

To make a fun party game, draw a large Allosaurus on sturdy cardboard and cut out the drawing. Then, cut out several tails for Allosaurus from construction paper. Tape Allosaurus to the wall. Give each of your guests a tail and a straight pin. Blindfold the guests, one at a time, and head them in the direction of Allosaurus. The player to pin the tail closest to the correct spot is the winner.

Find the rhyming words on the dinosaur fossils & write them in the correct spaces

Remember: the words at the end of each line must rhyme.

DINO-RHYME III

*By now you are nearly a dinosaur **wizard**,*
you can tell all your friends of the "terrible _____".

*What happened to them is a puzzling **question**,*
though scientists offer us many a _____.

60

Perhaps one day soon we will find a new **clue**,
the one to find the answer might even be _____ !

In section III you will have to use your **mind**,
to gain some "dino-info" of a very special _____!

TRICKY TRICERATOPS

follow the dots
to find Triceratops!

Many scientists believe that Triceratops may have been the very last dinosaurs to roam the plains of North America. Except for its enormous size, this triple-horned beast looked a lot like a rhinoceros. Triceratops looked fierce, but was actually only a plant eater who used small, sharp teeth and a powerful, parrot-like beak to chop and chomp plants. Although it is hard to believe, scientific findings indicate that Triceratops lived several million years after Brontosaurus.

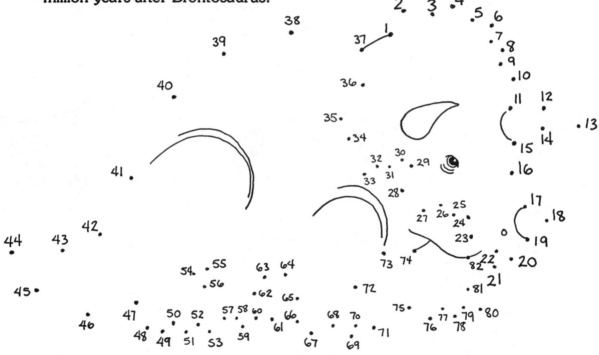

A MESSAGE TO DECODE

Work this code to find out about some other strange reptiles that lived during the same era as the dinosaurs.

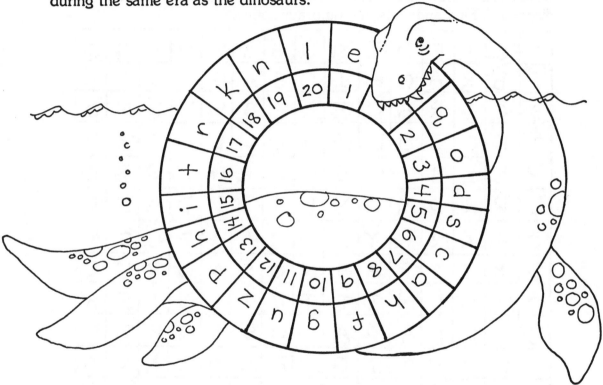

During the time that dinosaurs lived on the earth, strange animals lived in

the sea. They had $\overline{20}\ \overline{3}\ \overline{19}\ \overline{10}$ $\overline{19}\ \overline{1}\ \overline{6}\ \overline{18}\ \overline{5}$ that they used to

$\overline{6}\ \overline{7}\ \overline{16}\ \overline{6}\ \overline{8}\ \overline{9}\ \overline{15}\ \overline{5}\ \overline{8}$. They were called $\overline{13}\ \overline{20}\ \overline{1}\ \overline{5}\ \overline{15}\ \overline{3}\ \overline{5}\ \overline{7}\ \overline{11}\ \overline{17}\ \overline{5}$.

NAME THE DINOSAURS

The names of 10 dinosaurs are hiding in this word find puzzle. Some of the words read across and some read down, but none read backward or diagonally. Find and circle the dinosaur names.

P	O	T	E	D	I	M	U	H	A	R	P	E	N	D
E	B	R	A	C	H	I	O	S	A	U	R	U	S	L
D	C	I	R	A	C	E	R	E	J	W	E	R	M	O
I	H	C	S	O	L	M	A	D	U	L	O	E	R	D
P	L	E	S	I	O	S	A	U	R	U	S	O	B	O
L	P	R	D	N	C	M	E	N	I	P	D	A	J	C
O	F	A	N	K	Y	L	O	S	A	U	R	U	S	M
D	K	T	Y	R	A	N	N	O	S	A	U	R	U	S
O	N	O	D	M	I	T	T	Y	Z	O	O	L	E	W
C	A	P	L	A	P	A	T	O	S	A	U	R	U	S
U	P	S	U	T	I	G	E	R	L	A	S	K	V	A
S	E	G	S	T	E	G	O	S	A	U	R	U	S	Y
A	L	L	O	S	A	U	R	U	S	V	E	N	D	E
T	E	P	R	O	T	O	C	E	R	A	T	O	P	S

64

A "DINO" TEST FOR YOU

Use six of the dinosaur names hidden in the word find puzzle to complete these sentences. (When in doubt about an answer, be sure to look up the name in a reference book.)

1. _ _ _ _ _ _ _ _ _ _ _ was the longest dinosaur of all.
2. _ _ _ _ _ _ _ _ _ _ _ _ _ was a plant-eating creature that had an enormous head with three horns and a short, heavy tail.
3. _ _ _ _ _ _ _ _ _ _ _ was a reptile that had rows of razor sharp teeth, a long head, large mouth, and two hands with three giant fingers on each.
4. _ _ _ _ _ _ _ _ _ _ _ had big, bony plates covering its back and a spiked tail to swing at enemies.
5. _ _ _ _ _ _ _ _ _ _ _ _ _ _ _ was a huge and vicious dinosaur with long, sharp teeth and tearing claws. This dinosaur is said to have been the most powerful flesh-eating creature to ever walk on the earth.
6. _ _ _ _ _ _ _ _ _ _ _ has been called the "thunder lizard" because it made the earth shake and the trees fall to the ground when it walked.

It says here that this dinosaur has 3 horns & eats plants...

Then that must be the answer to # 2.

DINO-MAZING

Only one dinosaur needed to get to the sea . . .

It wasn't Protoceratops, a land-dwelling creature,
*   whose parrot-like beak was his outstanding feature,*
It wasn't Pteranodon -- or haven't you heard --
*   he flew through the air with the beak of a bird,*
It wasn't Stegosaurus, so slow and so fat,
*   with a long, powerful tail and a quite spiny back.*
Only one dinosaur had to get to the sea --
*   it wasn't any one of these dinosaurs three,*
It was duck-billed Anatosaurus who searched high and low,
*   for the water gave him food and defense from every foe.*

Help Anatosaurus find the water by tracing a path through the maze.

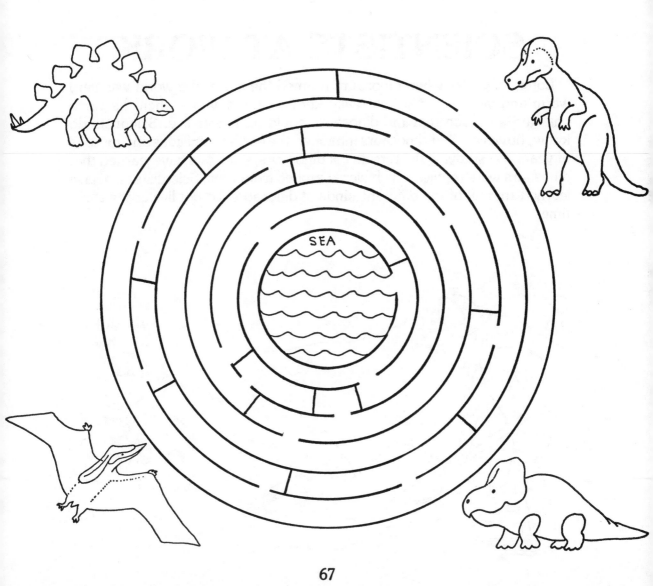

SEA

SCIENTISTS AT WORK

Long, long ago, when dinosaurs roamed the earth, the world was very warm and very wet. No one really knows why, how, or when the earth changed so much that the dinosaurs could no longer live. Scientists do know, however, that dinosaurs inhabited the earth for millions and millions of years. By studying the remains of dinosaurs, scientists have learned that dinosaurs were reptiles which were hatched from eggs. Scientists also have learned that all of the different kinds of dinosaurs did not live at the same time.

Scientists work hard searching for and digging up dinosaur bones that have been under sand and mud for millions of years. The places where scientists find dinosaur bones are the same places where the dinosaurs died. Scientists call bones that have turned to rock *fossils*.

After digging up the fossil bones, scientists carefully pack and ship the bones to a place where they can be put together, piece by piece. Putting a dinosaur skeleton together takes a lot of scientific knowledge, skill, and hard work. However, the scientists who study dinosaurs think that the hard work is worthwhile. It is through scientific study that mankind has learned about the prehistoric world.

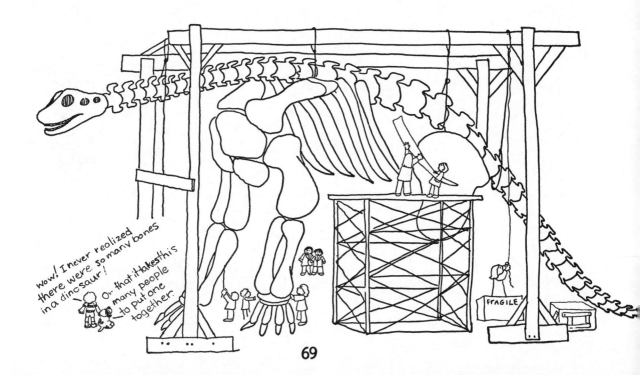

A DINOSAUR SKELETON

for you to disclose

Color the spaces numbered 2,4,6,8, and 28 to find a dinosaur skeleton under reconstruction.

DINOSAUR DIG

to see five dinosaurs below,
you won't need a shovel or pick,
crayons, markers, or colored pens,
will certainly do the trick!

Note: You may want to make your own hidden picture. Ask a friend to find and color the dinosaurs.

DINOSAURS ARE PUZZLING

to scientists as well as to you

Solve this puzzle to find the scientific name for a person who studies animals and plants of the past. To find the hidden word, carefully read each sentence below. If the statement is true, color the numbered spaces as directed. If the statement is false, color nothing.

1. If Ankylosaurus was an armored, plant-eating dinosaur, color the #1 spaces.
2. If Brachiosaurus was a small, meat-eating dinosaur, color the #2 spaces.
3. If Trachodon was a duck-billed dinosaur with webbed feet and lots of teeth, color the #3 spaces.
4. If Stegosaurus was a plant-eating, armored reptile, color the #4 spaces.
5. If Brontosaurus was a dinosaur of medium size with two feet, color the #5 spaces.
6. If Allosaurus was a fast and furious meat-eating dinosaur, color the #6 spaces.
7. If Diplodocus was the longest dinosaur of all, color the #7 spaces.
8. If Tyrannosaurus Rex was a plant-eating dinosaur who lived mostly in water, color the #8 spaces.
9. If Pteranodon was a winged reptile who soared through the air, color the #9 spaces.
10. If Triceratops was a giant dinosaur with five horns, color the #10 spaces.

I'd like to be one of these when I grow up.

I wonder if I could be a scientist's helper while I'm still a kid.

I wonder if cats can be scientists.

FOSSIL FINAGLING

Paleontologists study fossils to learn about animals of the past. Studies made by paleontologists have revealed that Anatosaurus, the duck-billed dinosaur, had lots of teeth. Use the code below to find out how many teeth Anatosaurus really had!

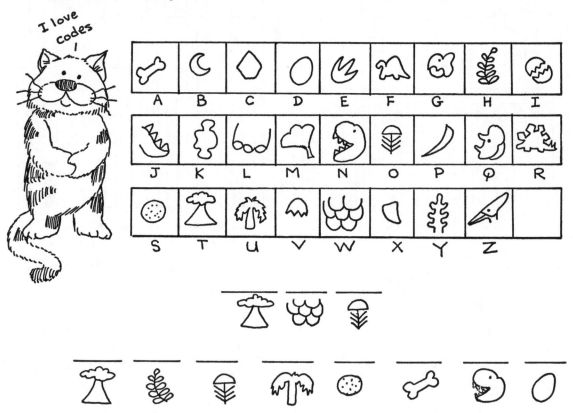

74

Geologists study the earth and its formations. Use the same code to find out how many years ago, according to geologists, the earth was formed.

This was *long* before dinosaurs lived on the earth.

Use the code to make messages of your own. Ask a friend to decipher them.

PUZZLE-O-SAURUS

a fun way to learn more about dinosaurs

DOWN

1. Dinosaurs lived _____ of years ago?
3. Baby dinosaurs were hatched from _____ .
5. Today dinosaurs are _____ .
9. A paleontologist studies dinosaur _____ .
11. Many dinosaurs had sharp spikes and horns to _____ themselves.
13. Brontosaurus hid from danger under _____ .
16. Would you have liked living on the _____ with the dinosaurs?

ACROSS

2. Pteranodon flew over the _____ .
4. Some dinosaurs were the _____ of a chicken.
6. Allosaurus hunted for _____ to eat.
7. Brontosaurus walked and shook the earth like _____ .
8. Some dinosaurs ate only _____ .
10. Ankylosaurus had bony plates all _____ its body.
12. Dinosaur means " _____ lizard".
14. Tyrannosaurus Rex had big, sharp _____ .
15. Most dinosaurs were probably brown or _____ .

ANSWER KEY

Page 63

They had long necks that they used to catch fish. They were called plesiosaurs.

NAME THE DINOSAURS

Page 65

1. Diplodocus
2. Triceratops
3. Allosaurus
4. Stegosaurus
5. Tyrannosaurus
6. Apatosaurus

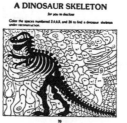

A DINOSAUR SKELETON

DINOSAUR DIG

Page 72

1.	true	6.	true
2.	false	7.	true
3.	true	8.	false
4.	true	9.	true
5.	false	10.	false

PALEONTOLOGIST

Page 74

two thousand

Page 75

four and a half thousand million years ago

INDEX